Breathing

Creating Spiritual Conversation in Groups

Mark Davis

Photographs by
Ged Barrow

Published by
Rockpool Publishing Ltd.
2b Marine Park,
West Kirby,
Wirral CH48 5HW
United Kingdom

ISBN 978-0-9554578-1-4

First Published 2008

Design and page layout Ged Barrow

Printed in Thailand

To Richard,
for faithful friendship, generous support
and valued encouragement

Contents

beginnings

In 1991 a charitable organisation was founded with the expressed purpose of responding to the needs of adult Christians to 'explore together what they experience and what they believe'. Called 'TIME + SPACE' it began as a piece of action-research looking at how, where and when this could best take place.

Over the next few years, informed by Carl Rogers' Person-Centred Approach and a spirituality of accompaniment, this ecumenical project piloted a new way of being in small groups. In a variety of settings, using different kinds of stimulus material, those involved gradually discovered for themselves the value of conversation as a vehicle for exploring the spiritual dimension to life.

The significant learning that occurred resulted, among other things, in a training process for the facilitators of such groups. This seemed both timely and appropriate as small groups are becoming ever more popular, both within the Christian Churches and beyond, as many of our fellow citizens again seek reasons for living and hoping. Less attracted to the formality of religious practice, they find in these smaller settings both spiritual nourishment and companionship – an antidote to the isolation and superficiality of contemporary society.

Although the 'TIME + SPACE' project came to an end in 2003, its contribution lives on. In recent years, through the development both of 'The Shoreline Consultancy' and 'Conversare', the work it piloted has found a wider audience. It now seems right, therefore, to respond to this growing interest and offer the fruit of this research and experience more widely. The publication of this book is one of the ways this is being attempted, as is the development of a project of the same name – designed to support the development of spiritual conversation in homes, schools and places of work or worship.

What is written here will be of particular interest to those who have been asked to accompany small groups of explorers seeking to grow in love and faith. It is not meant to be a substitute for appropriate training but could be seen as a sort of guidebook for those called to undertake this task. While its contents has been tailored to a particular way of accompanying others, experience suggests that the advice given here will be of value to anyone leading small groups gathered with a spiritual intention.

I hope that you will find the enclosed of value and that you will feel drawn to creating conversation and perhaps even joining what we hope will be a national association of friends and fellow travellers.

Mark Davis

N.B. By arbitrary convention, I have assumed in the text that all facilitators are feminine and that other members of the group are masculine - I hope this will not irritate or offend.

perspective

One of the most interesting paradoxes to have emerged within our culture in recent times is the increasing separation between spirituality and religion. While the former is enthusiastically sought, the latter is being avoided or rejected. Though one may debate the reasons for this, the persistence of interest in the spiritual dimension to living, highlights a basic human need - an awareness, a longing, a hope that there is more to life than meets the eye.

In my view this is more than aspiration or wish fulfilment. As the work of David Hay and others in researching modern religious experience demonstrates, experience of the spiritual is a part of everyday life. Unveiled in countless ways, which both energise and surprise us, we glimpse a loving guiding presence within, above and beyond the world. Though the busy lives we lead tend to conspire against it, increasing numbers of people are recognising the need to pay attention to these moments of insight and significance.

The problem we face is that we do not talk about such things with the freedom that we could, or should. In the normal round of social interaction, speaking of God has become almost a taboo. Cultural negativity reinforces a natural reluctance and so many feel unable to mention such things fearing misunderstanding or even ridicule. It is a sad fact that even many churchgoers rarely speak to one another about their spiritual experiences.

What we are beginning to realise is that in providing help for those who wish to converse in this way we need to intentionally create a particular kind of nurturing social environment – one in which people of quite different backgrounds and perspectives can feel safe enough to be real with each other about what they are experiencing and what they believe.

Over the next few pages I will be trying to describe in more detail the characteristics of this environment and how all this might be successfully created and supported.

breathing spaces

The title of this book has been especially chosen so to communicate a two-fold aspiration. The first is that the 'conversation groups' described within these pages will engender a profound sense of freedom. The intention is that they will be social environments of such quality that many who participate will experience a surprising sense of relief – that, at last, something they have wanted to do has become possible in a relaxed and comfortable manner.

My reason for emphasizing this point is that, as many of us realise, not all small groups gathered for religious or spiritual purposes are of equal value. At their best they can be immensely life-giving and faith-building; at their worst they can be manipulative, embarrassing and humiliating.

On many occasions I have had the privilege of seeing small group interactions of such quality that they have supported and encouraged profound, positive changes in the lives of those involved. Those who have found such environments helpful report a whole variety of beneficial outcomes. Some talk of being properly listened to for the first time or how they were able to experience a heightened sense of the presence of God. Others speak of how their mental horizons were expanded by listening to the wisdom and insight of other group members or of how such groups have been a catalyst to the healing of difficult relationships.

For many people such small groups have become oases of peace in their increasingly busy lives, places where they discover the joy of soul friendship and feel the support of others who share a common interest in the spiritual life. This can be particularly heart-warming when the sharing of personal experience reaches across the boundaries both between different denominational groups and beyond into wider society.

Sadly, examples of negative experiences in small groups are also not difficult to find. I have come across many people who have withdrawn from groups because they were made to feel ignorant or naive. Still more have felt pressured, judged or simply not valued for who they are or what they had to contribute. Such occurrences can be particularly painful if those concerned subsequently discover that what they had disclosed, in confidence, has been talked about elsewhere.

It hardly needs to be said that small groups are powerful social environments, particularly when they are designed as vehicles for exploring the spiritual dimension to life. Touching, as they inevitably do, the deeper parts of our experience, they need to be handled with sensitivity and care.

My second hoped-for-outcome in the groups we create is that there will be enough space in them for God to play. The Hebrew word for 'breath' is the same as for 'spirit' and if these conversations are to have lasting value, they must be open to what I would like to call 'the prophetic dimension'. While I would hope that we will all find being part of such groups enjoyable, let them not be so safe that we avoid the real challenges life experience invariably contains.

fundamentals

storytelling

Spiritual conversation in groups is grounded in the telling of personal stories – especially those in which the person concerned has managed to glimpse the presence and activity of God.   The opportunity is given to participants to sift through their own life experience and articulate what they consider significant as an offering for the enrichment of others.

Because of the subject matter, the term 'faith-sharing could be used to describe what goes on, though on some occasions it may be just as accurate to say 'doubt-sharing'. However, whatever is said, all responses are valid, for the intention is to create an open welcoming space in which people can share their insight and perspectives.

The wholesome energy that is created in such a setting comes not only from the stories themselves but also from the way in which they are received and respected.

heart journeys

Underlying the exchange, then, is a particular attitude and a way of relating – one which recognises a fundamental equality. Every member of the group is highly esteemed for who they are as a unique individual, not for what they are able to contribute. While some may have more knowledge than others, no one in the group is acting as 'an expert' – teaching things to other group members – like everyone else they are simply offering something from where they are on their journey through life.

In this kind of group, the articulate academic may appear to have an advantage, but his/her involvement in the group may be far less significant than the hesitant simple statements of someone less obviously gifted. The reason for this is that what is being shared is not a set of intellectual propositions, but an experience of life and a journey of the heart. What emerges comes not so much from sophisticated mental processes but out of a unique personal orientation to life and to God.

personal reflection

Implicit in this recognition is the observation that thoughtful spiritual conversation best arises out of reflective silence. For this reason the design of the small group process I will be recommending includes some time for participants to be on their own. The invitation is given to participants to stop and consider, in more than a cursory way, their own personal experience. Why this is so important is that only gradually, through taking time to reflect, will the deeper intuitions and meanings that you are carrying around be allowed to emerge. It is a valuable rule of thumb that 'the quality of the personal reflection dictates the quality of the subsequent conversation'.

For those who would like an image to conjure with, imagine that you are in one of those posh restaurants where you are presented with a large plate in the middle of which is a small quantity of expensive food. It would be foolish to dive right in and consume the morsel in one bite - far better to take a bit at a time and really savour the delicate blend of competing tastes and textures.

starting points

Another requirement, of course, is that there is something worth tasting to savour. This is not to imply that people will be short of relevant insight or experience, but just that it is sometimes difficult to access without assistance. I would suggest that some suitably engaging stimulus is required to get people started. It is very difficult to just turn up for a couple of hours one evening and begin to talk. Some prior planning and negotiation with the group are necessary so that something appropriate can be prepared. There are a whole series of possibilities available, some of which we will consider later in this book, but suffice to say that the group should try and identify for themselves the kinds of stimuli that encourages both personal reflection and later conversation.

striking a balance

As these pages unfold it will become clear that a delicate balance has to
be struck when designing environments to support spiritual conversation.
We will be hoping for freedom of expression, of course, and yet a
framework is required within which such spontaneity can flourish.
Certainly participants new to this activity can feel very uncomfortable
without an agreed form or pattern to the engagement. Nevertheless, this
'scaffolding' should not to be adhered to slavishly if the moment requires
a more flexible response. Over the years experienced facilitators have
found it most helpful to create a structured conversation within which
there are free flowing passages.

of conversation

Not everyone finds it easy to speak personally about the spiritual dimension to life and yet this is what makes groups of this kind so valuable. While not wishing to make anyone feel uncomfortable, we have to find ways of encouraging more than a superficial response to whatever stimulus is presented.

By the same token, not everyone listens well, particularly in a small group. It is not uncommon to come across individuals who find it very difficult to receive what they hear from others in a positive way - especially if what is said challenges their own deeply held opinions

a way of relating

Of particular importance, therefore, in groups of this kind, is the establishment of a way of relating which both invites significant exchange and also lessens our natural human tendency to descend into argument. Interestingly, such desirable qualities are enshrined in the original meaning of the word 'conversation' – which is why we have embraced the concept so warmly in our work.

According to the Oxford English Dictionary, the earliest understanding of the word 'conversation' comes from its Latin root where it implies a place of habitation, a home where those 'in conversation' share a common life. While it also records a whole raft of different meanings and usage (ranging in intimacy from the small talk of acquaintances to the delights of sexual congress) the thread of domesticity remains. According to the writers of the dictionary the transference of meaning from 'living with' to 'talking with', which occurred in both French and English, is a relatively recent interpretation.

The term identifies, therefore, a way of communicating which is both meaningful and homely. This we might expect, for it is only when we feel safe and 'at home' that we begin to disclose our real thoughts and feelings.

In my view, only when the risk is taken in the company of others to dive below the surface of the day-to-day can a 'conversation' be said to begin.

As we are beginning to see, the concept is so rich, that no single, simple definition will do it justice. It is better approached from a number of different angles as the following interwoven descriptors suggest.

A conversation may helpfully be described as...

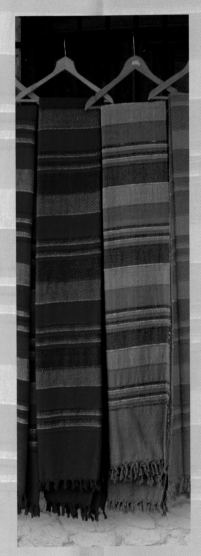

a verbal exploration of ideas, beliefs, values and meanings.

a meeting of hearts and minds where personal truth is shared and exchanged.

a place of safety where what is considered important has the opportunity to be spoken without fear of judgement, ridicule or recrimination.

an occasion of loving attention where whatever is said is received, reverenced and acknowledged.

a forum in which what is strongly believed may be gently challenged without fear or regret.

a place of risk and tentative personal disclosure.

an illuminated landscape where hopes and dreams are allowed to play.

an interpersonal journey undertaken by friends who are prepared to be changed by what they may subsequently discover.

what the educational philosopher Michael Oakeshott called, "an unrehearsed intellectual (and emotional) adventure".

a spiritual dimension

Because of the type of group we are considering, I take comfort in the fact that the word 'conversation' always seems to have had a spiritual dimension. Several writers are quoted in the dictionary as using the term to describe inward communion with God. One memorable translation from a letter of St. Paul, for example, proclaims that, "our conversation (i.e. our true home) is in heaven" (Phil 3 vs. 20).

If all this seems somewhat idealistic we should not feel alarmed. In the reclaiming of this word, we are holding up a vision of the kind of interpersonal encounter that people can walk away from feeling understood, accepted and affirmed. Though its full expression may be some way ahead of us, it is something towards which we can work.

discussion

Compare all this to the original meaning of the word 'discussion'. While it is often used synonymously with conversation, it comes from a very different root – the Latin word 'discutere' which literally means to "dash to pieces". A discussion, then, is not the coming together of those seeking understanding and communion, it is the clash of adversaries who wish to judge or examine an issue by argument.

In groups gathered to explore such sensitive issues as life experience and personal faith what we need to preserve is not a discussion, but a conversation. Together, in an atmosphere of trust and mutual respect we can speak about the spiritual dimension to human experience. We won't always see eye to eye, but we should be able to disagree gracefully.

life in groups

So far we have been simply concerned with the kind of exchange that forms the life-blood of this kind of small group. However, before embarking on any form of group work it is important to have some awareness of the nature of groups themselves. The first thing to realise is that any group worthy of the name is more than just a collection of individuals. It tends to function, in some ways, as though it was a living organism with its own life cycle and behaviour. It is not surprising, therefore, that people are affected by being in groups and their way of relating to others may change as a result. Some individuals come alive in groups - receiving energy and enthusiasm from the kind of social interaction they experience. Others find life in a group less pleasant and have greater difficulty in giving and receiving in this rather specialised environment.

key questions

In spite of these basic differences, however, most people struggle with similar unspoken questions when they first encounter a new group. Often revolving around issues of acceptance or procedure they include:

What are we doing here?
Who am I in this group?
Who else is here?
Who is in charge?
How will we operate?

Some or all of these questions may concern people at a first meeting; others may only emerge later; and some may be revisited on several occasions throughout the life of the group. Nevertheless, each of them must be dealt with, particularly at the outset, for their successful resolution is vital if the group is to develop into a productive and enjoyable association.

life cycles

Like a distinct organism, it is possible to chart the development of a group from its earliest beginnings to its ending. Extensive research into many different types of groups has resulted in several attempts to identify a developmental sequence. However, the one that is easiest to remember was suggested in 1965 by Tuckman who proposed the following progressive chronology for the different stages that commonly occur:

Forming

Storming

Norming

Performing

Adjourning

In the 'forming' stage people are concerned with learning about each other and with being accepted. They want to know more about the purpose of the group and how it is going to operate.

Once they have settled in, the differences in the group become more apparent and tensions arise. This may be no more than a disagreement about the timing of meetings, but it could be something more significant. There may, for example, be a strong challenge to the way in which the group is being led. For the facilitator, the focus moves to the management of this kind of conflict: hence the term 'storming'.

During the 'norming' stage differences are accommodated, a familiar pattern to the meetings is established and people become clearer about the purpose of the group. The 'performing' stage now has a chance to evolve in which the group functions in the way it was intended. In the spiritual conversation groups this is characterised by the development of sufficient trust for people to be able to speak from their hearts about faith and life.

The 'adjourning' phase is the process of bringing the group to a satisfactory conclusion. In my experience, conversation groups function best when they are designed to last for a limited number of meetings, contracted in advance by participants. Allowing a group to last beyond its sell-by date, can undo much of the good work that has been accomplished. Adjourning is best concluded with a celebration at which thanks may be offered for all that has occurred.

While they are undoubtedly useful, it must be remembered that Tuckman's stages are only approximations. Distinguishing clearly between them is sometimes difficult - they tend to flow into each other. Nevertheless, they remain valuable to the group facilitator who might, for example, be comforted to know that a certain amount of challenge to the status quo is not only to be expected but may actually be necessary if the group is to progress.

competing needs

Throughout the life of most groups a certain tension exists between three different but related needs. As well as the need for the group to achieve whatever task brought it into being, there are also the distinct needs of individual members. Added to this is the need to build up or maintain the group as a whole. Good facilitators will recognise the tension between these different needs and will attend to them appropriately.

As far as the individual is concerned, every participant comes to a group with a set of personal cares and expectations. During the life of the group these are played out. Whatever else concerns us we all need to feel accepted, valued and respected not only by particular individuals but also by the group as a whole. We also need to feel that the effort we are making to be part of the group is worthwhile and of benefit both to other group members and to ourselves. How we contribute and what we receive back will determine whether or not these needs are met and they will also have a direct bearing on whether or not the group stays together and completes what it was constituted to perform.

The relative importance of 'task' and 'maintenance' functions is dependent on the type of group and the reason for gathering. In many work-based groups the task is perhaps the most important element. The achievement of some common goal takes precedence over the needs of individual group members and the group is fostered as a unit in order for it to achieve what it set out to do. Conversely in those groups designed to foster personal growth, for example, maintenance becomes the crucial issue. Group identity needs to be encouraged and affirmed and positive relationships fostered.

In spiritual conversation groups, as I have described them, there is no set outcome decided in advance. The quality of the interaction is an end in itself. There are, however, many hoped-for outcomes. Through what is shared and explored, individuals may learn new things or gain new insights. They may be challenged or affirmed but it is hoped that any personal 'movement' will be in the direction of greater freedom, deeper faith and personal growth. Within such a setting, therefore, behaviour that contributes to the maintenance of the group also aids the task by helping to create the type of environment where the needs of individuals can be expressed and explored.

creating a helpful
environment

Spiritual conversation is a fragile plant, which needs a good deal of care and attention. So that it may flourish, a nurturing environment needs to be created which has a number of interlocking aspects, each of which we will briefly consider.

physical dimensions

Unsurprisingly, perhaps, the ease of conversation in this kind of group is influenced by its size. Experience suggests that an optimum number for such a gathering is between 7 and 12 people. This turns out to be large enough for participants not to feel 'put on the spot' and yet small enough to allow them sufficient 'air time' should they wish to contribute.

an appropriate setting

As we have already noted, the atmosphere in a group is heavily dependent on the way people treat each other. However, it is also influenced by the physical surroundings in which the conversation takes place. Too cluttered a setting, for example, can be very distracting to people who are trying to explore their inner thoughts and feelings. The size and shape of the room, its colour, warmth and odour can all make a difference to the way people behave.

Even things as simple as the placement of the furniture or the way a room is lit all have their effect. Arranging the chairs in a circle so that everyone can see each other is always helpful – but even here you have to be careful. They should be placed far enough apart so that group members will not feel on top of each other, but close enough to encourage intimacy. The seats themselves should not be so comfortable that they invite people to fall asleep but not so uncomfortable that they cause a distraction.

During the meeting, the lighting should not be too bright and it is preferable that it is flexible so that at different times in a meeting the room can be made lighter or darker. During a moment of prayer, for example, the lighting could be subdued, especially if a central candle is lit. At other times, such as during the offering of the stimulus material or the sharing and conversation, more light will be required.

a place on your own

An integral part of the process we are suggesting involves group members spending some time alone in silent reflection. While some people like to share these silent moments in company, others prefer to be on their own. Having somewhere for such individuals to retire to is not essential to the methodology, but it is a real help to those who need relative isolation in order to think.

It is worth paying deliberate attention to these details for what we are trying to create is a place where people feel at ease.

spiritual aspects

Many people can recall particular moments in their lives where they have felt the presence of the Divine. Further enquiry often reveals that this type of spiritual experience is closely associated with particular places. Most of us have a favourite type of place where it is easier for us to turn our minds and hearts to God. For some it may be old Church buildings or other formal sacred surroundings; for others some part of the natural world such as the coastal margins or forest glades. Celtic spirituality identifies these locations as 'thin' places where the distinction between this world and the next is somehow lessened.

When we are seeking to create helpful environments in which to engage in spiritual conversation we are left, it seems to me, with a choice. Either you gather in such places and allow the spaces themselves to inform your conversation or you try to recreate in your own environs a glimmer of what is found elsewhere.

thin places

This latter alternative will involve considering carefully what constitutes a 'thin' place. It may be the depth of silence, the background scents or the quality of light. Alternatively it could be something much more subtle – that indefinable quality to a place where people have prayed together for a long period of time.

While some of these things are impossible to reproduce, others can be attempted. Welcoming gentle music or the faint sound of flowing water can be very evocative, as can the subtle scenting of the room.

marking sacred space

To symbolically represent in physical form the theme of the conversation is a help to participants. In domestic settings this is particularly important as it marks out a sacred space for meeting. Always echoing the theme of the gathering, these simple three-dimensional works of art are designed to illuminate and resonate with whatever is presented for consideration.

The creation of a central focus is a wonderful opportunity for lateral thinking and creativity. It can be very simple or really quite complicated but it should not be too busy as this could distract and scatter attention rather than adding to it. It can, of course, be constructed of any mixture of materials but we have found that naturally occurring substances (e.g. leaves, flowers, rocks, shells etc) to be most engaging. Other useful examples include things made by direct human craftsmanship, as distinct from lines of mass production. Artefacts such as these retain something of the personality and individuality of their creator whether they are found in cloth, clay, wood or stone.

For those who find it difficult to express themselves in this way even a simple bowl of flowers, together with an icon or discrete cross placed on a coloured cloth, can make a tremendous difference to the overall atmosphere of the room.

the interpersonal climate

It will be clear from the last chapter that the way in which people can be encouraged to relate is highly significant in making a positive experience more likely. The particular way of being we are espousing is something we will be returning to in later pages, but there are one or two principles to the engagement which must be agreed by all participants at the outset. These principles could be identified as the norms of a spiritual conversation group as they express in microcosm 'the way we do things here'.

a shared commitment

The first has to do with confidentiality. For people to feel comfortable in disclosing what they would normally keep to themselves, an atmosphere of trust has to be developed. One of the most important aspects to this is the assurance that anything said within the confines of the group remains there. A commitment is required from all participants that nothing will be shared with others beyond its confines unless the person concerned gives specific permission.

appropriate self-disclosure

Just as important to ease in the group is a commitment to appropriate self-disclosure. We don't want to frighten each other, but we do want to communicate at a significant level. This means finding a suitable balance between these two extremes. If we disclose too much, we will not only embarrass the group but will probably regret it afterwards. If nothing personally meaningful is shared we have not really begun to converse and the whole experience will be unsatisfying.

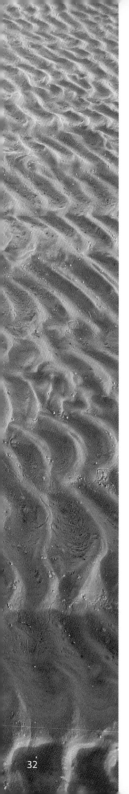

mutual respect

It goes, perhaps, without saying that personal criticism has to be avoided. Even if someone strongly disagrees with what another person says or believes, they must be encouraged to respond rather than react to what is said. I have found that a good way of responding in such a moment is to try and awaken one's own curiosity. "How can it be that this person believes what they do?" The effort to really understand where they are coming from can act as a useful restraining factor. It also communicates that most precious commodity – genuine respect.

settled membership

It will be clear that over the lifetime of a group the level of self-disclosure is likely to change. As people become more comfortable so they take greater risks in sharing. In many cases this adds depth to the conversation and thus increases it significance. However, if the make-up of the group is continually changing, the levels of trust and intimacy are affected. This, in my view, is reason enough to encourage a settled membership. While this is sometimes difficult to achieve, it is worth negotiating, particularly if the group is only going to meet for a limited number of occasions.

time boundaries

Agreeing time boundaries also affects in a positive way the interpersonal climate. If participants are not sure how long the session is due to last they may begin to feel uncomfortable. For the kind of group process we will be recommending approximately two hours will need to be set aside. If this seems a long time it is important to remember that the whole thing should not be rushed and spaces need to be found for people to sit and reflect. For some individuals, such sacred time and space is a rare and cherished opportunity.

facilitation

The creation of such a positive environment is best achieved when it becomes the collective responsibility of the whole group. However, it does seem to be necessary, especially when a group is forming (or is meeting only once) that a specific individual takes responsibility for how things develop. It is a time for sensitive leadership by someone who both models the best way of behaving, manages the interaction and looks after the developing needs of participants, particularly if they run into conflict. This type of leadership is often referred to as 'facilitation'.

We will be returning to the role of the facilitator in a later section but before we do, let us consider the kind of interaction she is hoping to facilitate.

structure
and
process

form and shape

Most people joining a group of any kind have concerns about the way it is going to operate. In the sort of group we are envisaging it is difficult enough speaking about things that are close to your heart without also having to worry about what might happen next. With this in mind I would like to suggest a particular methodology that you may wish to adopt. While not 'set in stone' it describes a well-tried small group interaction, which has proved very valuable in providing a context for spiritual conversation. It has enough structure to allow people new to this activity to feel comfortable and yet is not so confining that it prevents a meaningful response.

It may seem somewhat incongruous that something as essentially free-flowing as conversation should need some form of structure in which to flourish. Yet, we have found on many occasions, that this kind of temporary scaffolding is very helpful - particularly when a group is first forming. What it provides is both clarity and security for those participants who find the whole idea somewhat intimidating.

As the group matures it may well dispense with any kind of formal structure but its continued health seems to depend on the presence of certain key ingredients, each of which is set out in the 'model' process outlined overleaf.

preparation

prayer (prior to meeting)

preparation of the space

welcome and prayer

welcome and "how are you?"

shared silence and opening prayer

stimulus and reflection

introduction to the theme

stimulus material

time alone for individual reflection

sharing and conversation

the sharing of experience

conversation

review and prayer

looking back

shared silence and closing prayer

before leaving

refreshments & informal chat

Seen in summary form this group process appears deceptively simple. However, these brief titles require further explanation as each one is important.

preparation

Should you be asked to facilitate a conversation group, your involvement is likely to have three distinct phases – preparation, delivery and evaluation. The preparatory stage involves both remote and proximate aspects.

our need to pray

Facilitation of this kind of group involves making acts of faith - for no matter how skilled or prepared you believe yourself to be, a positive experience can never be assured. There are too many personal variables when a group of people whom you may not know well, start to open up to one another in your company. When faced with such a prospect, therefore, it is worth paying attention to the transcendent dimension to the encounter and prepare yourself appropriately. At such times we recognise once again our dependence on God and thus the staring point is in prayer.

For some readers it may be easier to think of this kind of preparation in another way. Most of us recognise the need to centre ourselves in the face of challenging circumstances. Before opening our doors and our hearts to others we should, therefore, seek harmony and balance within. Good facilitators will seek their own inner peace so as to be fully available to those they are about to accompany.

preparation of the space

The creation of a helpful environment has already been considered in a previous section but it is worth recognising that each individual session has its own tone. If the theme of the meeting is something joyous and relatively light-hearted, the choice of colours and music, for example, will mirror this subject matter. A very different physical environment might be appropriate to a theme echoing confusion, doubt or loss.

Thoughtful preparation of the space is a creative activity all of its own and you may find that it can be shared with other group members. Depending where the gathering takes place, the role of 'hosting' the group may be the responsibility of someone other than the facilitator. Clearly some kind of communication between the two is essential if a coherent experience is to be organised.

welcome and prayer

hospitality

The way in which people are welcomed is highly significant. Everyone needs to be assured that their presence is valued and this is especially so when they are meeting for the first time. We all have our own way of expressing warmth and interest but people quickly notice, for example, whether or not you remember their names.

introductions

After everyone has gathered it is often helpful to invite people to introduce themselves and say, in a sentence or two, how they are feeling. The point is made at the very beginning that the life experience of each person is of interest to the group and care is expressed for their well-being. Incidentally, the way in which the facilitator listens to these responses can set the tone for the whole meeting.

prayer

At this point a candle may be lit to signify a change of attention. The group is invited to become open to the silent, loving presence of the Divine in their midst. Should it be appropriate, this is acknowledged in a moment of vocal prayer.

stimulus and reflection

what kind of stimulus?

The choice of stimulus material is very much dependent both on the group concerned and the themes chosen to explore. Some groups gather around particular media, such as art, literature or film. Whatever is prepared needs to be of high quality, well presented and accessible to all participants. For many groups it is often helpful if there are choices, using different media, each of which illuminate a chosen theme. For example, a poem might be offered with a piece of Scripture, or some prose could be chosen to accompany a piece of art work. As a rule of thumb, the person choosing, either the facilitator or some other member of the group, should themselves be affected in a significant way by what they present to others.

engaging with this material

In general terms, participants need to be encouraged to connect with the stimulus material imaginatively rather than literally. A number of different ways of responding to it could be suggested but they should be more about 'sitting with' the stimulus and seeing what it does to you rather than trying to 'work it out'. Even when the stimulus is a piece of sacred text, the same invitation should be given.

personal reflection

It may be strange to suggest some time alone as part of a group activity and yet a period of silence (of perhaps 15 minutes) has two great benefits. Firstly, it gives time and space for God to speak in and through the reflective processes of each person. Secondly, it allows those who do not find it easy to express themselves in small groups, time to collect their thoughts and formulate a response.

sharing and conversation

rooted in experience

On returning to each other's company each person is invited to offer the fruit of their reflections. Everyone should be given the opportunity to share some of their thoughts, but there is no pressure to do so. Keeping in mind that the emphasis is on the sharing of experience, this will often take the form of a personal story in which some incident from their life will be illustrative of what they want to say. It may, however, be something else - perhaps the words of a song, a personal observation or just some nugget of wisdom or insight they have picked up on the way.

An image I have found to be helpful is that of people sitting around the tree sharing their Christmas presents. In this kind of circumstance most people recognise that the response to, "Look what I have got" is not a judgement or criticism but an attitude of interest and acceptance.

conversation

Once each person has had the opportunity of 'presenting', a more free flowing conversation may ensue when some of what has been shared is developed. Here the facilitator is at her most useful, paying attention to the group as a whole as well as to the individual concerned, intervening as appropriate to ensure clarity and kindness.

review and closing prayer

looking back

After an agreed length of time, there is silence once more as each individual is invited to make an internal review of what has taken place. The hope is that each participant will have found something to take away for further consideration. It is commonly reported that what emerges in the conversation group often sheds light on the time between sessions, making the series of meetings a coherent, collective faith journey.

Another aspect to this time of review is the opportunity it presents to care for one another in a deeper way. During each session there will inevitably have been a certain amount of self-disclosure and the invitation is given to each person to remember everyone else between meetings.

In this way one of the most valuable opportunities presented through this kind of encounter is made real in the widening of each person's circle of concern. We will all have discovered new things about one another – something which we can take into our prayerful moments. The risks that have been taken deserve this kind of loving response. If this dimension to the group experience is embraced wholeheartedly by participants it bears abundant fruit in the building of community.

closing words

At the end of this time of shared silence, should everyone feel comfortable with such an arrangement, a short vocal prayer (either prepared or spontaneous) brings the meeting to an end. Thanks are now expressed for all that has taken place.

before leaving

After such a group experience, which may last up to two hours, we have found it important that there is the equivalent of a 'warm down' after physical exercise - a time of relaxation accompanied by chat and light refreshments. This allows participants the necessary time to 'return to normal' before leaving.

the facilitative role

facilitation

The role of the facilitator in spiritual conversation groups is essentially two-fold: to both model an appropriate way of being and to 'manage' the conversation. In doing so she will be seeking to make it easier for participants to express their real thoughts and feelings. The facilitator is not 'leading' in the accepted sense but is simply providing a safe environment in which the group's exploratory conversation can take place.

to make easy

Now we have to be careful here for the term 'facilitator' is one of those titles currently in vogue and is found in a great variety of contexts. Different styles exist and these can hide different purposes and intentions. In these notes the word is understood in the way that is implied in its Latin root, 'facilis' meaning 'easy'. A facilitator is someone who tries to make it easy for others to successfully accomplish what they set out to do. In the case of the small groups we are considering, the desire of participants is to share their experience of life and faith. It is the task of the facilitator to help those involved find a positive way of relating, so that the truth they each possess may be expressed, appreciated and explored.

establishing norms

Having said this, at the outset of a journey with a group, the facilitator will be looked to for particular help in getting things started and in setting the norms for the interaction. Proper negotiation is vital at this stage, not only for the purpose of clarity but also because it can prevent problems later on. An early facilitative task, therefore, is to manage this negotiation. Once this has been accomplished and everyone is happy, a sort of unwritten contract has been established between group members, which will allow everyone to feel more relaxed. The naming of this by the facilitator on behalf of the group encourages a feeling of common purpose and co-responsibility for all that will occur.

This establishment of group norms (or common rules of the engagement) at the beginning of the life of the group also serves another purpose. One of the central challenges to a facilitator is how to intervene in moments of difficulty. It is very helpful if there have already been decisions made about how people will try and behave. Should they be breached, the door is open for the facilitator to remind participants, in a gentle way, of what they have previously agreed.

participation

As you can clearly see, a key issue in facilitation is the relationship between the facilitator and the rest of the group. Is she part of the group or detached from it? Should she contribute to the conversation or be somewhat apart? Should she express her own reflections or put them aside to concentrate exclusively on the facilitative tasks? In my view, facilitators of spiritual conversation groups should occupy the borderlands. They should be sufficiently involved so as to undertake the same risks of self-disclosure as anyone else, while remaining detached enough to intervene appropriately. The facilitator must recognise that it is not 'her group' - she is trying to establish collective ownership and responsibility. Others may look to her for expertise in the subject under consideration, but she must resist the temptation and remember that as far as the conversation itself is concerned, she is simply a participant.

a way of being in groups

Perhaps the most valuable contribution a facilitator can make to what happens in the group is to model an appropriate way of relating to others. There are many different approaches to facilitation but the way we are recommending as most appropriate and helpful, within spiritual conversation groups, is that which emerged out of the work of the American psychologist and therapist, Carl Rogers.

What Rogers called his 'Person-Centred Approach' came from a growing recognition that the best thing he could do to encourage positive change in his clients was to establish with them the kind of relationship they could use for their own personal growth. Instead of providing them with a solution of his own to their problems, he relied on their innate tendency towards growth and completion. Given the right interpersonal environment, he believed, they would find within themselves the inner resources they needed for their own healing. What he was trying to provide was a suitable facilitative climate.

the core conditions

Rogers' genius was his ability to describe such a climate
and how it could be created. Of crucial importance, he
believed, was that the counsellor or therapist acquired a
particular way of being with their clients. They needed to
embody an orientation characterised by three deceptively
simple ingredients. These fundamental attitudes
('congruence', 'empathy' and 'unconditional positive
regard') he termed 'the core conditions'. The following
brief description hardly begins to do them justice but may
provide a starting point for further research and reflection.

empathy

By carefully listening to someone it is possible to become
very familiar with their personal history. To truly
empathise, however, more is required. Only by being
sensitive to the feelings experienced by the other person
is it possible to recognise the world from their point of
view. While retaining a sense of one's own views and
values, to truly understand with empathy involves entering
imaginatively into their particular perspective.

As it will be appreciated, to see and feel things from the
standpoint of another is clearly demanding of both the head
and the heart. It requires acute sensitivity to their feelings
and thus makes great demands on our ability to listen, not
only to what is said, but what remains unspoken.

So delicate an attitude and understanding is rarely found
in full bloom but to be appreciated in this way, even
to a limited degree, is a liberating experience. Even if
such empathy proves impossible to attain in relationship
to another the effort itself is affirming for what it
communicates is profound appreciation and respect.

congruence

In everyday life people are very sensitive to a person's authenticity. We feel drawn to a genuine person. We trust them more easily than others who appear to be putting on an act. To be really genuine, however, is not as easy as it sounds. Everyone is tempted, at times, to present themselves as more knowledgeable or even more loving than they really are, particularly when operating in a professional context.

Rogers discovered that the more genuine he could be with his clients the more helpful would be the relationship. In his experience they were much more likely to achieve their own necessary authenticity when presented with a genuine, honest person. He recognised that it is no good presenting on the surface what one believes to be an appropriate attitude while feeling at depth something quite different. In his Person-Centred Approach there is no place for the professional façade. The counsellor, therapist or facilitator seeks to be transparent without pretence or defence.

The word 'congruence' is commonly used to describe this condition of genuineness. Rogers describing it on one occasion as "openly being the feelings and attitudes that are flowing within". What is implied here is that to be authentic it is necessary, among other things, to be aware at each moment of what one is feeling. It is not enough to be honest with the person in front of you, the challenge is to be honest with yourself.

Not that this is, in any sense, easy. The struggle to be authentic is an on-going process often punctuated with painful personal discovery. This perhaps explains why, of the three core conditions, it is often the most difficult to acquire and develop. Nevertheless its acquisition is of great value for a number of reasons. Congruence communicates respect of the other through the honest demonstration of interest and commitment. By the taking of responsibility for his/her own feelings the congruent person encourages others to do the same.

Two things, however, are worth noting to avoid confusion. Firstly, while cultivating an awareness of what is going on inside, a distinction must be made between what are fleeting emotional disturbances and those deeper feelings which remain within us for a significant time. Congruence implies paying attention to the second rather than the first. Secondly, awareness of one's own feelings does not imply that everything need be expressed. In some circumstances it may be necessary to disclose more than at other times. What remains constant, however, is the freedom to choose. The congruent person has sufficient self-awareness to be able to make the choice.

unconditional positive regard

The third core condition of Rogers' Person-Centred Approach is concerned with seeking to view those who are being accompanied as a people of worth. The term most often used to describe this attitude is 'unconditional positive regard' though some people prefer the more familiar, 'non-judgmental acceptance'. To regard another in the manner expressed here is more than a theoretical construct. It is a positive welcoming and valuing of the person. Some practitioners speak of it as personal warmth expressed in a 'non-possessive' way.

The word 'unconditional' implies that no matter what the person has done, how they present themselves or what they believe, they remain acceptable. For many individuals this presents a problem for they confuse acceptance of the person with 'approval'. Yet, as many parents faced with wayward children will attest, it is possible to have a very deep acceptance and love of someone without necessarily liking their attitudes or behaviour.

The danger, of course, is in pretending an acceptance, which is not felt. It sometimes requires a considerable effort to see beyond the unattractive appearance of the person concerned. For it to be possible it may be necessary for the counsellor or facilitator to make a profound act of faith.

What should encourage us, however, is the fact that the fruit of this gift of acceptance can be extraordinary, particularly in those who have experienced themselves as unacceptable whatever they do. Communicating a fundamental affirmation, it fosters a deepening self-worth and thus frees the person to approach the world with new confidence.

finding life

The relationship between the facilitation of spiritual conversation groups
and the Person-Centred Approach can, perhaps, be better understood
if you consider the following observations that have emerged from our
work.

In our experience such groups become life-giving...

*...when the group is experienced as a safe place. Only then will members
feel free to speak of the deeply personal concerns of life and faith. If
the facilitator holds the attitudes engendered by the core conditions and
she is perceived to do so, then group safety will be enhanced.*

*...when participants discover that they can be real with each other.
This can only take place over a period of time with the co-operation
of all group members but the facilitator, in trying to be a model of
authenticity for everyone else, can be highly influential. If she is seen as
transparent, genuine and to some extent vulnerable, the group is given
permission to be the same.*

*...when group members have learned to trust each other. Again this is
a gradual process but as far as the facilitator is concerned she must be
perceived as someone worthy of trust. Openness and honesty should
characterise their behaviour in the group as well as their own trust of
God, the group and the process in which they are engaged.*

*...when individual participants feel valued for who they are. The
welcome given to all participants must not depend on the depth or
frequency of their involvement in the group. The facilitator has
an important role to play in valuing each person for who they are.
Regardless of whether or not individuals choose to speak during the
meeting each person is thanked for being present and thus contributing
to the life of the group.*

...when each person feels accepted and acceptable. In spiritual conversation groups people will undoubtedly be at different places on the journey of faith. It is vital for their freedom and growth that they are made to feel that wherever they are is O.K. Some people find this very difficult to accept. They feel a great urge to correct those who do not agree with them. The facilitator needs to protect group members from judgmental interventions of this kind.

...when individual participants feel understood. At a deeper level than simply the intellect, those who contribute need to feel that others are attentive to their unique experience. In this way the rest of the group prizes their contribution. Again the facilitator plays a key role in receiving, sensitively and thoughtfully, what they have shared.

...when there is a positive response to the involvement of feelings. For many people it seems as if religious teaching, often in philosophical or 'drained language', has thwarted the interaction between genuine feelings and faith. Being able to express emotion about these things and having it received in a positive manner can be profoundly affirming.

If such are the characteristics of the group and the way it interacts participants experience a great sense of freedom. They become more able to explore; to share; to make mistakes; to change their minds; to express their emotions; to admit doubt and fear; to listen to others and learn from their experience and insight; to engage thoughtfully with the story of their faith community and see where it leads them.

Suffice to say that behind this way of operating in groups is a very optimistic set of assumptions about the nature of human life and our trust in the kind purposes of God. The demands made of participants, particularly the group facilitator, could be expressed as several interlocking acts of faith:

Faith in the inner resources of the individual; faith in the resources available to the group as a whole; faith in the process of their involvement and, most of all, faith in the loving presence and activity of God. Over the years, in making these acts of faith, we have not been disappointed.

the skills of a facilitator

It is out of the way of being previously described that the skills of a facilitator emerge. Rather than appearing stilted or forced, the way she manages the group, intervenes or responds flows naturally from one aspect to another. The group should feel 'held' not in a controlling way but lightly and yet with assurance.

listening

One of the key skills of a good facilitator is her ability to listen. This is partly about paying careful attention to what is being said but it is not simply a passive receiving of information - it is a much more active process. Particularly in the context of a small group, no matter how much a person needs to speak, it is difficult for them to keep going if they are not receiving anything back from the listeners. What is required is sometimes called 'helpful responding' – the use of short phrases, non-specific noises or body language to communicate back to the speaker that they have been heard and understood. A positive comment here, a sympathetic noise there, appropriate smiling, eye contact or gestures of concern all help to assure and encourage. Though only one person is speaking there exists an on-going subliminal dialogue, which provides a supportive emotional context in which real communication can occur.

Successful positive listening demands the ability to be present, to live in the now - focussed entirely on the one who is speaking as though they were the most important person in the world. To achieve this requires both desire and concentration. You really have to want to hear what they have to say and you need to make choices that make it more possible.

attending

Part of the skill of listening is the ability to communicate easily and
successfully that you are following and are interested in what the
other person is saying. This can involve responding verbally but just
as important are the non-verbal messages that accompany all we say.
Whether we like it or not these present our feelings to the other person,
either reinforcing or undermining what we are saying.

While some people wish to train themselves to send appropriate
non-verbal messages, I have my reservations. It appears somewhat
manipulative to artificially reproduce these non-verbal signals.
What is more useful is to learn to pay attention to your own body, thus
bringing to consciousness the messages you are naturally sending. This
gives important clues to your own levels of concentration or attention.

noticing yourself

It may seem something of a paradox but while listening to others you also
need to be aware of what is going on in yourself. If the words of another
have any meaning at all they will affect us as we hear them. Such effects
will be noticeable in mind, heart and body. You may find that what is
said triggers thoughts and images in your own mind - things that have
happened to you, things you believe, questions you have. Just as easily
your emotions may be stirred as you imagine what the other is feeling
and it resonates within your own personal history.

The truth is that our bodies react in noticeable ways to what is being said. For example, no matter how hard we try, sometimes we begin to feel restless and physically disturbed when listening to someone. Our mind or will may say that we should ignore such things and concentrate, yet the message from our body is that we can't do it anymore. On such occasions it may be necessary to acknowledge the fact, apologise and try to discover what your body is telling you.

tone and texture

As we are all aware, good listening involves more than just hearing the words, it also includes observation and interpretation. The pitch, tone and texture of the human voice adds to the subtlety of the language and the body provides other non-verbal clues. What is often not recognised, however, are the changes in energy that accompany different parts of a conversation. Facilitators need to be aware of such things if they are to be effective. Sometimes, of course, it is the silence between sentences that speaks most clearly of what occupies a person's mind. What they choose to avoid in conversation may be very revealing.

peripheral awareness

One of the challenges to facilitators of groups is both to pay close attention to the person speaking and yet also be aware of what is happening, at the same time, in the rest of the group. This noticing of the others demands something I like to call peripheral awareness. Similar to the concept of peripheral vision, it suggests being open to the emotional and physical responses of other participants as they listen to the person sharing their experience. Things like shuffling are very obvious manifestations of unease, but it is also possible to recognise tension, boredom or embarrassment in a group. A good facilitator will try to be poised within the group, ready to respond to unspoken signals as well as more obvious methods of communication.

ready to listen

In spite of our best intentions, it must be admitted that, even the best facilitators are not always ready to listen. I find it important in preparing to facilitate groups that I spend some time on my own. In my experience, to listen properly to others I have to feel relaxed. This involves my becoming quiet inside. Leaving aside those things that may be causing inner disturbance is never easy but it is a necessary exercise prior to attentive listening. Tension can, of course, come from many sources but there is one source of anxiety that is often overlooked. In a strange way good listening is often related to how at ease you feel in talking about yourself. Concern about how you are coming across in the group and what you are going to say next can get in the way of your listening.

intervening

One of the most common questions from those being trained in facilitation concerns intervention. Where, when and how should a facilitator enter the conversation? The first thing that needs to be said is that intervention is a much wider term than is commonly thought. Whenever a facilitator speaks about the life of the group she is intervening. These interjections are much more commonly to provide information, or to make suggestions, than to avert some difficulty or danger.

Let us consider the methodology outlined in a previous chapter:

> *preparation*
> *welcome and prayer*
> *stimulus and reflection*
> *sharing and conversation*
> *review and prayer*
> *before leaving*

It will be clear that interventions by the facilitator will include the introductions and connecting sentences that will help the group to move easily from one stage to another. For example, the group will be invited to spend some time in silence before sharing their responses to the stimulus. The facilitator as well as giving her own contribution to the conversation may wish to summarise what has been previously shared.

when to intervene

Where interventions are more common and, of necessity, more spontaneous, is when the sharing and conversation takes place. It is hoped that such interventions will become less and less necessary as the group develops but they may be required in some or all of the following situations:

An individual wants to speak and is not being given the opportunity.

Certain group members are losing interest.

A monologue or dialogue develops which excludes other group members.

The group becomes tense or embarrassed.

Factions begin to emerge.

Whispering takes place.

The conversation stays entirely 'in the head'.

Someone is openly criticised.

The conversation drifts into argument.

When relevant information is required and it isn't forthcoming.

'Red herrings' are introduced.

People keep repeating themselves.

The group appears confused.

should I intervene?

If you have time to weigh up the possibilities you may want to consider the
following:

> *What do I want to achieve?*
> *What will happen if I don't?*
> *What effect will my intervention have on group members?*

The decision itself cannot be anticipated and there is always an element of
risk when intervening particularly when responding to moments of conflict.
Everyone makes mistakes and there is no substitute for having a go.

how to intervene

Over a period of time people develop their own style of facilitation and this includes their ways of intervening. In general terms, however, I offer the following guidelines:

Interventions are best made in the form of questions or suggestions.

A brief review of the developing situation is often helpful.

Naming your own feelings is often important as it invites others to do the same.

An element of humour is sometimes helpful in diffusing tense situations.

If you have to interrupt do so with due deference and an apology.

You may need to remind the group of agreements you have previously negotiated.

Whatever style and use of language you develop, it is important to remember that every intervention is an act of love on behalf of the group. The role of the facilitator is to make it easier for participants to do something they may find difficult – communicating freely about spiritual things. In the heat of the moment what is sometimes required is the balm of a calm, assured presence. At such times the facilitator has the opportunity of proving her worth.

dealing with conflict

In groups, conflict can range in intensity from mild disagreement to aggressive confrontation. Fortunately, in conversation groups, the latter is quite rare, but should this be the case the following advice may be helpful.

Whatever the cause of the conflict it is usually best to confront it rather than let it fester. In actual fact the outcome from such an event may turn out to be beneficial to those involved. We must accept that there may be a risk of damage to relationships and therefore the trust and goodwill of the group. It is just as possible that a successful resolution of these difficulties will lead to greater intimacy and trust as well as the emergence of unlooked-for creative opportunities.

In dealing with conflict, should it become more threatening to the group than the expression of differences of opinion, the following procedures could be adopted...

...Express your concern: explain the reason you wish to attend to the situation and bring the problem into the open.

...Seek clarity: try to describe the different positions being adopted by protagonists for the benefit of the whole group.

...Check the feelings of others: attempt to discover whether other group members, not directly involved, feel as you do about the situation.

...Invite suggestions: allow the whole group to come up with ways of resolving the difficulty.

...Seek agreement: involve not only the protagonists but also the rest of the group.

suitable training

For most people, the need for a certain amount of training in facilitation
is most evident when considering both intervention and conflict
resolution. Structured practice sessions are immensely valuable in
developing the necessary confidence and expertise. So too is thoughtful
consideration of the underlying attitudes necessary to communicate a
positive response when faced with new and challenging situations.

images of facilitation

To illustrate further the role of the facilitator it may be helpful to paint one or two pictures. Below are a series of images, each of which throws light both on the nature of facilitation and the tasks the facilitator is required to perform.

beachcomber

One of the most evocative images of the faith-sharing group is that of a group of friends walking together along a beach. On their way, as well as sharing stories, they drink deeply from their surroundings, looking around, listening and breathing in the living air. The shoreline is a borderland where the sea and the land encounter one another, a vibrant symbol of the relationship between the physical and spiritual dimensions of reality, an interface between two worlds. The beachcomber is familiar with this place and has made a habit of examining and exploring what is left on the beach by the retreating tide. To those with whom he walks he points out, in the flotsam and jetsam, things of interest which have tales to tell about life in the sea.

contemplative

Good facilitation is about awareness - both of oneself, the group and the relationship between the two. A contemplative is one who observes not in a superficial or detached way, but with a gaze that looks both here and beyond. He is a seeker sifting through his experience for understanding and insight, gently pondering and savouring what comes to his attention. Acquainted with mystery he finds great wonder in much that others would dismiss or ignore. Quietly, with reverence and respect, he looks upon the world with spiritual eyes.

gatekeeper

In both the monasteries and walled towns in the Middle Ages the gatekeeper was of great importance. He acted as a guardian to those inside, checking the boundaries and making sure that they were not breached or compromised. His primary task was to ensure the safety of those in his care.

sacristan

Often called a sexton in the English Church, the sacristan is one who is given particular responsibility for the fabric of a church and its contents. Preparing and keeping a sacred space for the use of others is his primary function. Often overlooked, the care of the building and its preparation as a place both of worship and silent welcome is a creative and valuable ministry. In protecting and presenting this physical environment the sacristan gives important messages about the beauty and majesty of God and the welcome given to all.

fathomer

In the days of sail when wind-powered vessels carried men across the oceans to chart and explore newly discovered lands it was the duty of the fathomer to measure the depth of the water. Plumbing the depths, as it was called, provided, vital information particularly around uncharted coasts where hidden reefs might cause a ship to run aground. On such occasions he was constantly alert, monitoring the situation and ever ready to assure or to warn about impending difficulties.

accompanist

During a recent concert at which a marvellous tenor enthralled the audience with the beauty, control and quality of his voice, it was difficult not to be struck by the invaluable contribution made by his accompanist. The initial timing of each piece of music was hers, as was the underlying texture of the performance, yet as the tenor took centre stage she bowed to his mood and intention, subtly improvising in response to his lead. Her undoubted talents could have gone unnoticed but without the musical context she provided, the virtuoso could not have expressed himself with the same passion or assurance.

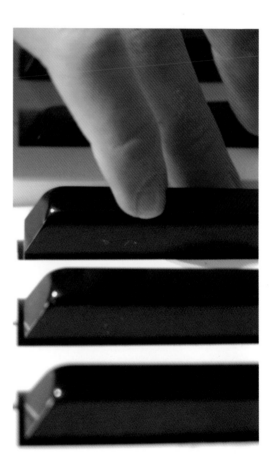

how to start
your own group

what do I need?

The place to begin when considering starting your own group is to ask yourself what you need personally to make a good job of it. Have you the time, interest and commitment to see it through? Does your personality equip you naturally for the role of facilitator, or would you benefit from some training?

You may be someone with lots of previous experience in similar kinds of settings. If so, these notes may simply remind you of what you already know and suggest a particular methodology you may wish to adopt.

However, if this kind of activity is new to you – but you already see its value – why not try it out among a few friends? Look upon it as a shared exploratory activity, adopt the group process we are recommending and trawl around for suitable stimulus material.

The following pages outline the steps that we have found helpful in establishing a worthwhile conversation group. Some, or all of them, may be relevant to your situation.

gathering a group

Having decided that you are ready to proceed, the first challenge is likely to be gathering your group of fellow travellers. Much depends on whom you have in mind. Are they people already known to you or are you hoping to attract a wider constituency? What shared interest or experience of life has the potential for drawing them together?

Our experience over fifteen years suggests that the energy needed for gathering groups comes from at least four different directions:

particular media

Some people are attracted to a certain medium of expression such as art, music, literature or simply the experience of the natural world. It is through the experience of this media that they commonly look below the surface of life to find its spiritual dimension.

shared concerns

Other individuals gather because of a shared interest - perhaps the faith-life of their children; or concerns about justice in their own locality and the wider world.

professional development

Some people working in Church schools or sharing some ministry in the local church often recognise a need to gather for reflection and spiritual conversation. This is partly motivated by the desire for mutual support and the need for a safe place to take their own issues of life and faith.

a desire for spiritual formation

Others simply wish to enter more deeply into their spiritual lives, perhaps responding to an inner call. Sometimes the desire to explore further is prompted by significant life events such as bereavement or the birth of children.

It is probably important on a first occasion to choose a reason for gathering that sits most easily with you and try and match it up with those you are hoping to invite. What tends to happen is that once two or three people have become interested in forming such a conversation group they themselves often persuade others to become involved. In spite of the new technology, word of mouth remains the most frequently successful method for initiating a first meeting.

introductory meeting

When enough people are forthcoming (perhaps 8-12) arrange an inaugural meeting to discuss what is possible and whether or not what is proposed conforms to their needs and interests. The subject matter of such a negotiation has been alluded to on previous pages but suffice to say that there needs to be great clarity about the terms of a person's involvement in a spiritual conversation group.

Most people need to retain some control over their level of commitment. It is helpful to have built-in escape routes for those who find that, having turned up, it is not what they were looking for.

where and when

Where groups meet can be highly significant. Again it depends on who wishes to become involved. Some groups are best formed in a domestic setting and this might be particularly useful for welcoming those who have no formal religious commitment. Others meet in different locations depending on the stimulus material chosen. We have seen successful groups meeting in Art Galleries, in rooms attached to pubs, and even outside in public gardens or by the sea.

Times of meeting can be problematic as many people lead such busy lives. Evenings tend to be favoured by most groups, though groups of mums or retired people often gather during the day. If, because of time pressures you may only be able to meet occasionally, at least try and put the agreed dates in the diary.

The length of time between meeting does have an effect on the cohesion and sense of identity engendered in the group - but you just have to negotiate what is possible. Anecdotally, meeting every two weeks seems to work best from the perspective of group development, though meeting every month is also workable.

within your Christian community

Suppose, rather than operating independently
you wish to facilitate conversation groups within
you local church? In many churches there exists
a pressing need for its members to find a way
of speaking gracefully to one another about life
and faith. Should you wish to bring spiritual
conversation to bear on this problem, how is it
best approached? Clearly the approval of your
minister or priest will be important, but even
with their support you will still need a good
method of introduction.

Our experience suggests that it is often helpful
to present your fellow church members with an
opportunity to 'sample' what is being offered.
After outlining to the Sunday congregation the
basis of the approach and the need for faith-
communities to converse in this way, a general
invitation could be given to a 'taster afternoon'.
This might take place on a weekend afternoon
within a couple of weeks of the invitation.
Those who choose to attend can experience a
typical session. Should enough people wish to
take matters further a negotiation takes place in
which they can decide how to proceed.

the negotiation

As I have mentioned previously, the value of this activity cannot be overestimated, but how shall it be undertaken? The first thing to note is that negotiations take time and cannot be rushed. With this in mind I would tend to spend the whole of a first session reaching a suitable consensus. The issues under consideration would include:

clarification of purpose

This may seem unnecessary but it is worth checking. It needs to be established that the gathering is, first and foremost, an opportunity to share experience in response to the stimulus provided rather than anything else.

a way of relating

Mention should also be made of the nature of conversation and agreement reached about the keeping of confidences, appropriate self-disclosure and the avoidance of personal criticism.

methodology

Explaining what will happen when and why is also necessary so as to overcome feelings of unease among participants. Time boundaries should also be negotiated.

suitable stimuli

It is worth enquiring of the group what types of experience awakens in them a desire to consider the spiritual dimension to life. For many people it is important life events, such as bereavement or becoming a parent. For others, the medium might be more important than the occasion – so that it is engaging with art, reading particular authors or listening to music which acts as a doorway to the interior life. Good facilitators will take these matters into consideration when choosing suitable stimulus material. Arriving at attractive themes and presenting engaging stimuli is a challenge in itself.

practicalities

Often the most difficult bit of the negotiation is agreeing on the practicalities of meeting together. How many times should we meet? How often? When and where? As a guiding principle, we should always negotiate a precise number of meetings with the group concerned. Because this way of relating takes time to internalise, I would recommend no fewer than three meetings and preferably between seven and ten – after which there should be an evaluation process.

accompanying the group

Once a group has started, participants may be quite happy to let you, as the facilitator, shape the way forward. The choice of session themes and the finding of suitable stimulus material will probably be your responsibility. Over time, however, as everyone becomes more familiar with the process, it is usually beneficial to let other group members contribute to the creation of individual sessions. They may wish to choose themes, provide the stimuli, prepare the place of meeting or even host the exchange. The more participants begin to feel a sense of ownership for what takes place in the group, the greater likelihood is of their appreciation and commitment.

As far as the facilitator is concerned, your direct involvement should diminish as the group matures. A good test of the success of a conversation group is the way it begins to run itself and how often the leadership tasks are undertaken by a growing number of participants. There may come a point where it no longer needs to be accompanied in the way it was at the outset.

between meetings

It is frequently reported that what emerges during such a gathering
has a richness which is hard to take in all at once. The invitation has
already been given within the meeting itself to review what has taken
place, but there is still a need to process its significance. Participants
in conversational groups of this kind are encouraged to record their
thoughts and feelings in a spiritual journal. This personal diary allows its
author to look back after a series of meetings noting points of growth as
well as memorable insights. In doing so the fruit of the encounter may be
better integrated into the pattern of our days.

learning from experience

The process of evaluation is a vital tool for learning and developing as a facilitator. Throughout the lifetime of the group a good practitioner will be evaluating all that occurs and at the end of the agreed number of sessions will be asking the group to evaluate for themselves what they have experienced. This on-going evaluation tends to take two forms for at the end of each session it is important to examine both what happened in the meeting itself and your own performance.

With regard to an individual session try and look back over the meeting and see if you can identify moments of ease and moments of difficulty. Consider what you have discovered about the group as a whole and the different participants, their history, needs, engagement or expectations. How will this information help you in planning for the next meeting?

When evaluating your own performance recall how you felt at different stages in the meeting. Can you remember moments when you felt either comfortable or the reverse? What do you think caused these differences? What are you discovering about yourself and your abilities as a facilitator.

evaluating the whole process

Any notes that are taken after each session will also inform the reflections of the facilitator about the whole journey. She will have been able to note attitudinal changes in the group, significant learning, difficulties and their resolution. These observations are worth pulling together prior to the final meeting at which evaluation will occur. It is best to have something to refer to should it be required.

It is sometimes advantageous to prepare an evaluation sheet with questions to guide the group's reflections of the group as a whole. The fruit of this enquiry should be talked through as a whole group so that everyone can learn from the activity.

training, referrals and support

learning opportunities

I hope it will be clear from what you have read in this work, that the facilitation of small conversation groups is not beyond the scope of many people. However, it is not for everyone and many who do have the necessary natural gifts still require help if they are to facilitate effectively.

Suitable training may be accessed through 'The Shoreline Consultancy' (www.theshorelineconsultancy.co.uk). On-going support, connection and attractive resource material can be sought from 'Conversare' - the spiritual conversation place (www.conversare.org.uk).

referrals

Anyone undertaking this kind of ministry, as well as receiving adequate training, should be aware of the limitations to their involvement. People come to such groups with a wide variety of needs and expectations some of which are beyond the scope of this kind of setting.

Sometimes, during the course of a meeting, it becomes clear that what a particular person needs is not spiritual conversation but actually counselling or psychotherapy. Facilitators should have at their disposal the names and contact details of other professionals able to offer this help. They should not take on people or situations for which they are not qualified or competent to manage.

personal support

It is also important, I believe, that trained facilitators have their own network of support and/or supervision - people to whom they can go for advice or encouragement. A local group of facilitators may wish to get together at intervals to share insight and experience as they grow in this ministry.

facilitators checklist

preparation

readiness

Are you satisfied that you have enough relevant prior experience to feel comfortable facilitating this group?

Have you taken the opportunity to acquire sufficient training to facilitate such groups in an assured and confident manner?

Is this a good time for you to be facilitating this group - mentally, emotionally, physically and spiritually?

Have you enough time available to devote to this task, so that you can give of your best?

partnership

Do you prefer facilitating on your own or would you benefit from working with someone else?

In looking for a co-facilitator, what skills, qualities and knowledge will you seek that will balance or complement your own?

How will the different duties of hosting and facilitating be apportioned in the place you have chosen to meet?

remote preparation

How will you go about gathering your group? What shared desire or interest will encourage them to meet?

Have you decided on a suitable location? What will you be looking for in terms of space, facilities and atmosphere?

facilitators checklist

preparation

Are you clear about your role in relation to the group as well as the nature and purpose of spiritual conversation?

How confident are you in negotiating with the group? What are the norms and boundaries you will be seeking to establish?

chosen themes

Are you comfortable with the overall theme you have agreed with the group as a stimulus to conversation?

Have there been any related events in your life, which remain sensitive areas for you and still need addressing?

Can you foresee any potential areas that may cause you to become unsettled and inhibit your role as a facilitator?

proximate preparation

How are you going to make the place of meeting as welcoming, comfortable and relaxing as possible?

What kind of central focus will you prepare to symbolically echo the material the group will be considering?

Have you gathered together all the things you will need to facilitate the group effectively e.g. leaflets, pens, prayers etc?

Have you remembered to pray about the group itself, the needs of individuals and your facilitative role?

facilitators checklist

delivery

welcome and prayer

How will you make sure that you extend an equally warm welcome to every participant?

In inviting those present to speak about how they are feeling, how will you be seeking to communicate acceptance and understanding?

Are there any previously negotiated agreements that are worth revisiting with the group at the start of the meeting?

How will you encourage participants to recall the presence of the Divine? Do you need to prepare a prayer for use at the beginning?

stimulus and reflection

How will you go about introducing the theme of the meeting in a way that is understood by everyone and is open to exploration?

Is the stimulus material you will be providing open and inclusive? Does it reflect the capabilities of the group?

Have you made sure that there is enough varied stimulus material to cope with the different learning styles of participants?

Will it be possible for people to 'get away' from each other to reflect on their own prior to engaging in conversation?

facilitators checklist

delivery

sharing and conversation

How will you remain engaged with the group, fulfilling your role but retaining your personal integrity?

In what ways are you prepared to support those who may find some aspect of the gathering uncomfortable?

How will you make sure everyone has a chance to contribute and what strategies will you adopt to deal with emphatic or intransigent positions?

What methods of conflict resolution are at your disposal, should this aspect of facilitation be required?

review and closing prayer

Will you be able to give participants a brief overview of the themes of the conversation and the way it unfolded?

How will you express gratitude to the group for their participation in the meeting and their contribution to its value?

Have you prepared a final prayer or reflection? How will this enshrine or imply gratitude to God for making the gathering sacred?

facilitators checklist

evaluation

of the meeting

How do you feel everything was received and did people feel able to contribute honestly?

To what extent did participants respond imaginatively and creatively to the stimulus material that was provided?

Have you a record of key ideas to remember as part of your introduction to the next session?

of your role

How did you find the whole experience? Is there anything you would have done differently if you had to repeat it?

Did you manage time-keeping effectively, beginning and ending at the agreed times without appearing rushed or unsettled?

What have you learned from this experience about facilitation that would be useful to you in the future?

by the group

At what stages are you going to invite participants to evaluate their own experience of involvement in the group? Will this be done verbally or in written form?

Do you need to prepare a suitable evaluation sheet for use at the end of the agreed number of meetings?

How will you process, record and learn from the information you receive without betraying any confidences?

Bibliography

Bausch, W. J: *Storytelling, Imagination and Faith*
                 Twenty-Third Publications 1988

Bozarth, J: *Person-Centred Therapy: A revolutionary paradigm*
                PCCS Books 1998

Davis, M: *Walking On The Shore.*
                Matthew James Publishing 2002

Gallagher, M.   *Free To Believe*
                Darton, Longman and Todd 1996

Guenther, M: *Holy Listening*
                Darton, Longman and Todd 1992

Hay, D: *Religious Experience Today*
                Mobray 1990

Johnson, D. W. & F. P   *Joining Together*
                         Prentice-Hall Inc. New Jersey 1975

Nelson-Jones, R: *Human Relationship Skills*
                    Hold, Rinehard & Winston 1986

O Murchu, D: *Reclaiming Spirituality*
                Gateway 1997

Peck, M Scott: *The Road Less Travelled*
                  Century Paperbacks 1987

Rogers, C. R: *On Becoming A Person*
                 Constable 1967

                 A way Of Being.
                 Houghton Mifflin 1980

                 Freedom To Learn.
                 Bell and Howell 1983

Thorne, B: *Carl Rogers.*
              Sage Publications 1992

              Person-Centred Counselling and Christian Spirituality.
              Whurr Publishers 1998

about the author

Mark Davis

Mark Davis is founder/director of The Shoreline Consultancy - an ecumenical organisation dedicated to 'supporting and developing Christian communities'. He is also a member of the Spirituality Committee of the Roman Catholic Bishop's Conference of England and Wales. Over the last fifteen years Mark has been invited to deliver his own unique blend of consultation, facilitation and training within a variety of ecclesial contexts both in this country and abroad. In doing so he has undertaken projects on behalf of the Methodist and Anglican Churches as well as contributing to the strategic development of a number of Roman Catholic Dioceses and Religious Orders. Recognised as an accomplished facilitator of large gatherings - such as the provincial chapters of religious orders - he has also acquired considerable expertise in the creation and sustained development of small groups. Holding out a renewed understanding of the nature of conversation, he trains facilitators to accompany such groups in a wholesome, life-giving way. Of his own developing interest in this area he writes:

"As I look back on my own faith journey I am deeply indebted to those fellow travellers, both men and women, who found time to speak to me at a significant level about the spiritual dimension to life. Such was the value of these graceful encounters, that I became convinced of the value of conversation as a way of nurturing and sustaining faith. In these sacred moments I glimpsed the power, presence and love of God and was assured of his kind purposes both within the details of my own life and in the lives of everyone else. It was this gradual unfolding, echoed in my own experience of prayer, which shaped and continues to shape the direction my life has taken".

For more details about Mark's work or to make contact visit:
www.theshorelineconsultancy.co.uk

about the photographer

Ged Barrow

Ged Barrow has been described as a "Contemplative Photographer". He has worked closely with a broad range of spiritual and religious organisations and is a director of Rockpool Publishing. On Photography he writes:

"As a small boy I discovered that once you have fully connected with the practice of looking at life as if through a viewfinder, the habit never quite leaves you alone. As I see it therefore, the main requirement for being a creative photographer is to fully engage with life.

We live our lives through a series of present moments. The past is only a repository for memories, and the future a storehouse for dreams. The 'now' is where we actually live. Yet we spend so much of our time regretting rejoicing, worrying or expecting...dreaming of a future as yet unlived, attached to a past already over.

For me being in the now brings a sense of connection with the world as a place of extraordinary miracles, often played out graphically through a 'conversation' between light and shadow. The discipline and challenge for a photographer is simply to remain sufficiently present in and awake to the performance that life is constantly playing out in front of us.... and with good fortune occasionally press the button at the right moment".

If you wish to see a gallery of Ged's images, find out more about his work or contact him, visit: www.gedbarrow.com